How Animals Play

How Animals Play

Betty Tatham

Franklin Watts
A Division of Scholastic Inc.
New York • Toronto • London • Auckland • Sydney
Mexico City • New Delhi • Hong Kong
Danbury, Connecticut

To our grandchildren: Sarah, Jenny, Mary, and Stephanie

Note to readers: Definitions for words in **bold** can be found in the Glossary at the back of this book.

Photographs © 2004: Animals Animals: 46 (M. Colbeck/OSF), 45 (Howie Garber), 6 (Gerard Lacz), 11 (A. & M. Shah), 38 (J. & P. Wegner); Corbis Images: 35 (James Marshall), 24 (Stuart Westmorland); Dembinsky Photo Assoc./Fritz Polking: 37; Minden Pictures: 21 (Tui De Roy), 5 left, 51 (Mitsuaki Iwago), 23 (Mark Jones), 29 (Flip Nicklin), 19 (Michael Quinton), 32; National Geographic Image Collection/Tom Murphy: 16; Peter Arnold Inc.: 52 (Auscape International), 47 (Denis-Huot/BIOS), 9 (Norbert Wu), 40 (Gunter Ziesler); Photo Researchers, NY: 27 (Tim Davis), 10 (Gregory G. Dimijian), 36 (Gilbert Grant), 49 (Jeff Lepore), 2 (Renee Lynn), 13 (Tom McHugh), 5 right, 42 (Yva Momatiuk & John Eastcott), cover (Art Wolfe); Visuals Unlimited/Joe McDonald: 48.

The photo on the cover shows two grizzly bears play fighting. The photograph opposite the title page shows cheetahs at play.

Library of Congress Cataloging-in-Publication Data

How Animals Play / by Betty Tatham.
    p. cm. — (Watts library)
Summary: Discusses different ways animals play and explores the significance of these activities. Includes bibliographical references (p.) and index.
ISBN 0-531-12173-9 (lib. bdg.)   0-531-16236-2 (pbk.)
    1. Play behavior in animals—Juvenile literature. [1. Animals—Play behavior.] I. Title. II. Series.
QL763.5.T35 2004
591.56'3—dc22

    2003012578

Contents

European wolf cubs enjoy some playtime.

Chapter One

What Is Animal Play?

A young male wolf paws at another pup's face. Then he races off and returns quickly to face the other pup. He runs back and forth several times, as if to invite his brother to chase after him, but nothing happens. Finally, he crouches down with his forelegs stretched out on the ground and his hind legs stand straight up. He waves his bushy tail from side to side. This is a **play bow**, and now the two pups race off and take turns chasing each other.

Most animals use play signals to let another animal know that they only want to play rather than fight. They usually have another signal that tells the play partner that they have had enough and want to stop. Some wolves, coyotes, and wild dogs may also perform a play bow in the middle of playing, to tell the partner that "this is still play." This happens most often right after play biting, which could be misinterpreted as an aggressive action. The play partner who bites gently without closing its teeth together, will often shake its head from side to side, signaling that this action is still play.

Why Animals Play

Like humans, other animals play because they enjoy the play activity. Playing is done for the sheer fun of it. There is no other purpose or goal. Playing just feels good.

Play can, however, have other benefits. It can teach skills that will be used later to escape a **predator**, to hunt for food, or to increase strength and endurance. Playing can also help animals to make friends with others in their group.

Playing is usually done in a relaxed way. Most often, it is done more quietly than fighting, which may be accompanied by loud howling or screeching. However, some animals squeal with delight or make other noises that show how much they are enjoying a play activity. Doglike **canines**, such as wolves, and some other animals have a relaxed grin or friendly "play face" during play.

Three Kinds of Play

There are three kinds of play. **Motor play** is play with movement where muscles are used to run, jump, kick up heels, do somersaults, climb, twist, dance, twirl, and do many other play activities. Most animals do this type of playing without a partner. Benefits of motor play include strengthening muscles and practicing maneuvers that build skills. These actions will later be used in self-defense, such as jumping up and kicking heels at an enemy. Some actions will also be used to escape a predator or to capture **prey**, such as twisting, twirling, jumping and climbing.

    Object play is similar to human play with toys. Objects or things used by animals in play include pebbles, sticks, shells,

Bottle-nosed dolphins are extremely playful, engaging in activities such as jumping out of the water.

bones, a dried leaf, a snowball, a feather, dead or live prey, and many others. While humans are likely to store and keep their toys, most animals just find new ones each time they want to play. Objects are handled, thrown, dropped and caught, balanced, rolled, juggled, pounded, bitten, and pulled away from another animal. Most object play is done alone, but sometimes two animals play tug-of-war with a stick or other object that they both want.

There are many benefits to object play. Animals that learn to pick up sticks and other objects may later use these skills in nest building. By picking up objects and carrying them some distance using grasping and holding techniques, animals learn how to better handle their prey. Learning to retrieve a dropped object will later help in recapturing food.

Two cheetah cubs play tug-of-war with a hat that had blown off a man's head. The former owner of the hat watched from his vehicle while the young cheetahs played with their new toy.

The third kind of play is **social play** in which two or more animals play together or in a group. Play fighting, boxing, wrestling, chasing, fleeing, kicking, butting, hitting, racing, chasing, pushing, and other types of social play help animals to get to know each other and to build friendships. They also strengthen muscles and build skills that will help in a real fight for a mate or with a predator. Social play teaches tactics that help to capture and hold on to prey or to escape an enemy. By playing with each other socially, the young of a family group get to **bond**, or care about each other. This may later motivate them to fight bravely to protect the whole group from outsiders.

While two young cheetahs rest, a third cheetah prepares to pounce and engage in play.

11

Play between animals of unequal size and strength is not unusual. In such cases, the stronger animal will hold back and not use all of its strength with the smaller or weaker play partner. If this didn't happen, smaller animals would probably not agree to play with stronger ones. So even when two animals are not well matched in size, speed, or strength, the stronger one will let its play partner win some of the time.

Play Is Not Meant to Be Hurtful

Play activities are not intended to hurt or kill another animal, and they usually don't. Play provides opportunities for physical exercise that strengthens muscles. Play activities also teach strategies that may help an animal capture prey, avoid or escape from a predator, or defend itself against an enemy.

Play is also distinguished from fighting by its many interruptions. The stop-and-go of play adds to the excitement and slows things down when a play contest gets too competitive. In a fight, on the other hand, the two enemies will fight to the finish, when the loser leaves or is killed.

While play fighting may serve as practice for escape or defense against an enemy, it can also be preparation for later sexual activity. For instance, playing rats often nuzzle each

Play Is Good for the Brain

Some scientists, especially psychiatrists who have studied animals, feel that playing helps to develop the brain. In fact, these scientists believe that not being able to play may be harmful to animals, including humans. Most animals that play have well-developed brains.

other's necks, an activity that is also performed before mating. Sea otter pups play chase with each other. A pair of adult sea otters may play chase for several days at mating time.

In a real fight, an animal has to attack and defend itself at the same time against the next blow or bite from its opponent. In a play fight, animals rarely attack and defend at the same time, and they allow some blows to hit them without blocking them. A play fight is similar to a boxing match in which each animal tries to gain the advantage, but where there is no desire

Two young rats cuddle in a corner during play. Many young animals learn about their own body and the bodies of other members of their species during play activities.

to knock the opponent out. In an uneven match, where one animal is much stronger, it will usually **self-handicap,** or use only part of its strength, to let the play partner win some of the time.

In some species play fighting can become a real fight, such as in hamsters that are about to become sexually active, or in coyotes and wolves that are old enough to fight for the leadership position. In most species, play fighting does not escalate into a real fight, unless one opponent constantly blocks the other animal from striking back.

Some scientists believe that play fighting can teach an animal not to be afraid to strike back after being attacked. It also teaches animals that play with live prey how to interact with the captured animal.

Young Animals Play Most

Most play activities are performed by young animals, before they are old enough to mate and breed. Only humans and a few other species, such as apes, elephants, and dolphins, continue to play as adults. Adult animals usually play less than they did before becoming sexually mature.

Since young mammals drink their mother's milk, they have more time to play than other animals that must spend much of their time searching for food. The mothers of young mammals also tend to keep them nearby and to watch over them, making it safe to play. Since most birds are also fed and watched over by a parent, many species of birds play when young, and some continue to play as adults. Even though animals play because they enjoy doing it, play activities help prepare them for adult life.

Ravens and crows like to play in the snow. After pushing some snow around with its beak, this young raven ate a mouthful of snow.

Chapter Two

Birds at Play

Black wings stretched out, a crow glides toward an old barn and lands at the top of its snow-covered roof. It lies down on its back, feet forward, and slides all the way down the side of the roof. Once in midair again, the bird flies back to the rooftop for more sledding. This time its mate also joins in.

Crows and their raven and magpie relatives are especially playful birds. They have been observed sliding down snow-covered hills and roofs only to walk or fly back to the top for another fun ride in the snow. Some will do this play activity several times, so sledding may be as much fun for them as for human children.

Playful Crows and Ravens

Crows and ravens also like to bathe in snow. While adults bathe only once a day, younger birds may do it several times a day and for longer periods. They also like to bury play objects in snow. One raven was seen poking a long stick into the snow until it couldn't be seen any more. Others hide food in snow or under leaves. While these birds don't seem to care if other birds see them burying a toy, they will fly out of sight so that others can't see where they hide food.

Ravens mate for life. Sometimes mated ravens hold claws for a short while while flying. One bird will fly in the usual position, while its mate flies lying on its back with claws pointing upward to grab those of its partner. When chasing each other, ravens take turns in the chase. They can do **rollovers** while in midair, and they like to **dive-bomb**, flying straight down very fast and stopping just a foot or so before hitting another bird or the ground.

Ravens have been observed hanging by one claw from a branch while holding a stick in the other claw. They then pass that stick to their beak and back again to the claw. They also like to drop sticks, rocks, or other play objects in midair and swoop down to catch them. Sometimes one bird will drop an object and another will go catch it.

Beginning and Continuing to Play

Ravens may begin playing with sticks in the nest even before they can fly. They continue to play with objects all of their lives. Young birds are, however, more adventurous in finding new objects to play with. Adult birds tend to play only with familiar objects, such as those they played with when younger.

Crows and ravens play "pass the stick," where the bird with a stick in its beak is "it" until another bird pulls the stick away. Then that bird becomes the one pursued by the others. In flight, these birds often move a stick from their beak to one foot, then to the other foot, and back to the beak. One raven

This photograph shows two ravens in a play chase. Ravens also like to play drop-and-fetch games.

Tricky Birds

Crows and ravens especially like to tease other animals. A crow may peck at a wolf's head or tail, then fly away while the barking wolf races after it. Some crows have a favorite wolf to play this trick on. Crows have also pecked at resting deer, ridden on the back of a **boar** or wild pig, and played with or pestered other animals.

was seen hopping on one foot while dragging a rock with the other foot to the edge of a cliff. Then it pushed the rock over. It repeated this play activity with several more rocks. Ravens also play fight while lying on their sides and kicking at each other. Sometimes, one will jump on its play partner's back.

Other Birds at Play

Hawks, eagles, and owls play with objects that can't be eaten as well as with dead and live prey. They toss or drop an object and chase after it, catching it with their beak in midair. These and many other birds also like to play chase each other.

Warblers, finches, and parakeets play with small stones or feathers, which they drop and catch. Woodpeckers fly at each other, chase and dodge, beak wrestle, and pull each other's tails. Parrots nip with their beaks to start a play fight.

Adélie penguins play "king of the mountain," with each penguin wanting to stay on the highest spot. The one who becomes "king" is soon pushed off, and another penguin will briefly hold the coveted spot. Peregrine falcons hold play battles in midair that prepare them for real battles with predators like adult eagles.

Hornbills like to **jostle** for position. Two young hornbills sometimes wrestle on the same branch, pushing each other and jabbing gently with their beaks at the play partner. Some also pull each other's tail feathers. Hornbills and many other young birds perform gentle play fights while still in the nest, and some like to tease each other.

Two sea gulls may play tug-of-war in the air with a strand of seaweed or a stick. Gulls also like to fly holding objects they can't eat, then drop them. Some dive after a heavy object that they dropped, then fly under it and straight up to catch it. These antics may help gulls to drop clams from some height to break them open on rocks below to expose the food.

In Antarctica, these Adélie penguins engage in some social play on an ice floe. Once they are in the ocean, however, predators— such as the leopard seal in the foreground—hunt them for food.

Chimney swifts play "drop and fetch." After dropping a stick into a stream, they fly down and fish it out. Then they drop it again and do the same thing several more times. Frigate birds play follow the leader, with a line of birds diving down toward tidal pools and stopping just before they reach the water, then soaring back up again. They may repeat this behavior around a number of different pools. Sometimes one bird will drop a piece of seaweed and another will swoop down and catch it before it hits the ground. These and other play activities help these birds to hone their skills in swooping down to grab food out of a tidal pool or the ocean, and in recapturing food that has been dropped.

Birds That Make Snowballs and Other Play Activities

Young keas in New Zealand are very playful. They enjoy several different play activities. They do somersaults on branches and also in the water. They may swim on their backs. Keas sometimes hang upside down from branches while holding on with their claws. They also like to play with snow. They make and push snowballs with their beaks. They sometimes walk stiff legged on the ground, prancing in front of a play partner, as if they were marching in a parade. Keas can lie on their backs and juggle or balance a stick or other object with both feet in the air.

While play activities are performed because they are enjoyable, they teach and improve a variety of flying, catching,

passing, and other skills and they increase muscle strength. Tactics learned in play can be useful in many ways, such as helping a bird escape a predator, catching prey, hanging on to it in flight or recapture it, and making prey accessible by opening the shell that protects it.

A kea in New Zealand has been manipulating a small stick with its beak, before burying it in the snow. Keas are exceptionally playful birds.

Harbor seals are very playful marine mammals. Here they rest between play bouts.

Chapter Three

Play of Water Mammals

Two young harbor seals romp in the water near a small rocky island. They form a circle with each pup's nose next to the other's tail. Both are splashing and thrashing about. After a short rest, they repeatedly leap out of the water onto rocks, then fall backward into the ocean. They blow bubbles and throw pieces of **kelp** or seaweed into the air with their snouts. Then one pup jumps on top of the other and they playfully twist their necks around each other. After all this

frolicking, they tire and then rest peacefully, floating next to each other at the water's surface with eyes closed and cheeks touching.

Play in the Ocean

Many species of seals play in pairs or groups. Sometimes an entire herd plays together on a rocky island or shore, with some seals hopping out of the water, then diving on top of others as they swim by. When tired out, they move to higher ground and rest until every member of the group is sprawled out on rocks.

Sometimes a fur seal pup will grab a strand of kelp between its teeth and quickly swim away from other pups. These other pups then chase after it. As soon as one of the pursuers manages to grab the kelp away, the others race after the new "it." Gray seals do somersaults in the water. They also chase each other and do head shaking.

Sea lions, walruses, and seals all like to play while young. Some of these pups first play with their mothers, while others play mainly with other pups. Play fights may include pushing, shoving, grabbing, or shaking. Steller sea lions especially like

Studying Animals at Play

Scientist Robert Fagan, author of the college-level textbook *Animal Play Behavior*, studied wild animals at play in Alaska for more than ten years. He feels that play helps animals learn how to make good decisions, prepares them for life as adults, and is an activity they do because they enjoy doing it.

to bite their play partner and then try to escape before being bitten in return. Walruses play mainly underwater where it's easier to move their large hulks. Mock battles are their favorite play activity.

Elephant seal pups play in groups or pods. When they are about one month old, they are left alone by their mothers, which go into the ocean to feed. The young pups stay close together on land. They spend a lot of time splashing around in tidal pools, where they learn to swim. They often pile on

Two young male elephant seals are mock fighting. As adults, they will use these skills to compete for a harem of cows, or female seals.

top of each other on the beach, making a small hill of brown furry pups. When they are three months old, their new silvery fur coat has grown in, and since this fur is waterproof, they can now go live in the ocean.

Another marine animal, the manatee, is also very playful. Manatees like to dive, splash, chase, and wrestle with each other. Calves twist, tumble, bump each other, and barrel-roll. They also kiss, nuzzle each other, and hug while playing.

Sea otters play with their food. They also like to box, tumble, and tease each other. They romp and play chase both underwater and at the surface. Sometimes one sea otter hides and then pops up suddenly to surprise its play partner.

Whales and Dolphins at Play

Humpback whales **breach** by rising out of the water, head and body held high, then falling back onto their side. This may be a type of play activity, but no one really knows for certain. Sometimes a mother and her calf will breach at the same time, or a male and female will breach together before mating.

Many times, sperm whales have been observed surf riding, or tumbling and diving under a plank of wood, swimming away and returning to dive again. A captive orca whale was seen picking up a round floor brush at the bottom of its pool and then swimming with the brush balanced on its head. Orcas are social animals that hunt in groups. However, not much is known about their play behavior in the wild.

Gray whales are playful. More than a dozen mothers and

Is It Really Play?

Some scientists have guessed that humpback whales breach because it helps them to shed barnacles that have attached themselves to their large bodies. Other marine biologists feel that barnacles are **imbedded** in the skin of whales and can't fall off. They think that whales breach because it is a fun activity, similar to dolphins jumping out of the water. No one can be certain why whales leap out of the water, but people love to watch them do it.

calves can play together, rubbing against each other and rolling around in the water. Young calves also like to pick up kelp with their noses and swim around with it.

Bottle-nosed dolphins are extremely playful water mammals. They often play chase and frequently play with one or more particular play partners. They have highly developed brains and exceptional learning and communication abilities.

Study of Creative Play Activity

A study of two bottle-nosed dolphins in an aquarium observed their ability to make bubble rings with their flukes and then move those rings around as toys. Seven different ways of playing with the bubble rings were noted, and the calves often copied each other's actions as they moved the bubble rings around.

In captivity, bottle-nosed dolphins perform in many aquariums. They easily learn to bounce balls, toss rings, ring bells, manipulate various types of toys, and do other tricks on command for a food reward. While these activities can't all be classified as play since they are not performed just for the fun of it, dolphins do play with objects by themselves and with others while in captivity, even without being rewarded with food.

Bottle-nosed and other types of dolphins like to jump out of the water often. They also enjoy riding the big bow wave of ships or waves left behind by large whales, and they surf ride and play "approach-flee" games. Divers have also been approached and nudged by a dolphin, until they stroked the dolphin. The dolphin obviously enjoys this playful interaction.

Mammals That Play in Rivers and Lakes

Similar to sea otters, young river otters are also playful. They like to slide down muddy banks, climb back up and do it over again many times. They also enjoy play chasing.

Young beavers are also very playful water animals. Beaver **kits** wrestle and push each other on the shoulders with forepaws while standing on hind legs. They roll around together, tumble, and do somersaults in the water. Beavers live with their parents until they are about two years old, and they are playful throughout that time.

Whether young mammals live in freshwater or in the ocean, those with parents who look out for their young and who also have well-developed brains, tend to be playful. Some play with objects, such as bubble rings or pieces of kelp, and others prefer motor play, swimming under or around things many times, or sliding down a riverbank. Many water mammals are active in social play in pairs or in groups.

Protected Young Animals Play More

Animals raised by their parents for a long time, tend to play more than those that become independent soon after birth. A young animal that does not have to spend much time hunting for food or protecting itself will have more time for playing.

A young patas monkey is waiting for its play partner to join in play activities.

Chapter Four

Primates Play Most

Chin on the ground, hind legs standing straight up, a young patas monkey looks up at another **juvenile**. This play invitation is accepted when both race off. They chase each other through tall grass, often bouncing high up and down.

Suddenly both monkeys run at full speed, and each hurtles itself at a bush, grabbing it with both hands and feet. They bounce off in a new direction and run farther before grabbing another bush and repeating this exercise. While zigzag running may be a fun play activity for these young monkeys, it can also save their lives. Predators are usually unable to change direction so quickly, making it harder to catch the monkeys.

While a juvenile may bounce up and down in tall grass for the fun of it, this activity can later benefit the clan of monkeys. When a lion comes near a group of patas monkeys, the adult males start bouncing through the tall grass to distract the lion and draw its attention away from the females and their young. When the lion chases after one of these males, the monkey may be able to zigzag run to safety.

Patas monkeys may invite each other to play by bouncing from their feet to their hands and then back and forth. This also helps develop bouncing skills. They play wrestle by trying to throw each other off balance and may slap at each other playfully with their hands and may also play bite.

Monkeying Around

Monkeys are often associated with playfulness, so much so that the phrase *monkeying around* describes playful or mischievous behavior. Young rhesus monkeys spend most of their time either playing or sleeping. Their play signals include swaying from side to side with their head hanging down near the ground. Another play invitation is a staggering walk, followed by a roll over onto the back with all four limbs in the air. These monkeys may also use a play bow and friendly play face to show that they are ready to play.

Species of Primates

There are close to three hundred species of apes, monkeys, and **lemurs**. The number of species varies because new species are discovered while other species are endangered. All of these mammals belong to the group called **primates**, as do humans. Primates are a group of mammals with highly developed brains, forward-looking eyes and well-developed hands.

Rhesus monkeys live mainly on the ground, but they also play in trees, chasing each other. They especially like to make their play partner fall. Knowing how to fall can be helpful in fleeing from a predator. These monkeys like to whirl around fast, do back flips, and play hide-and-seek. The hiding monkey crouches down in tall grass and doesn't move until another monkey comes quite close, then it runs off and hides again. Learning to hide from a play partner can be helpful in escaping an enemy, or in hiding and then surprising prey.

Rhesus monkeys also play "king of the mountain" where the king tries to stay on a tree stump, while the other monkeys try to push him off so that they may become the next king. They also jump off trees into the water, making belly flops, and sometimes they jump near or on top of another monkey, pushing it under. They like to swim underwater and to splash a lot. Adults play less than juveniles, but they continue some play and swim activities throughout their lives.

A rhesus monkey is hoping to start a play chase up the tree.

Some Males Play More

After they are six months old, male rhesus monkeys play more than females, and they play more aggressively. This helps them prepare to fight other males for a female partner as adults.

More Monkey Play

West African guenon are monkeys that live in trees and like to chase squirrels and annoy birds. Young guenon scare hornbills away from their nesting sites by shaking branches at them. After fleeing, the birds return, only to be driven off again until the monkeys tire of this game.

When spider monkeys play fight, one may bite the foot of the play partner and that monkey will then bite the head of the first monkey. Neither tries to stop the other's biting. Their open-mouthed, grinning play faces show that they like this activity.

Callicebus monkeys are small, and they make a big game of protecting their territory. Each morning after breakfast, the parents and their young go to the edge of their territory and

Spider monkeys are playful acrobats.

In northern Japan, a young macaque, or snow monkey, plays with a snowball it has made.

wait for their neighbors. As soon as the neighbor family has arrived, the monkeys purposely put their feet just inside their neighbors' territory. The shrieking and arguing over this offense can last for hours, but there is never a real fight. When they get hungry, everyone leaves to eat, and the game is over until the next morning.

Langur monkeys do handstands while playing. They also race up a tree and fall down backward from the top, grabbing at branches as they fall. Once at the bottom, they climb back up to repeat this game.

Japanese macaques are monkeys that make snowballs that are as large as a baby's head. They roll a snowball on the ground, and they also like to carry one around as a play object or toy. Sometimes two macaques put their snowballs together, and they have also been observed jumping on their snowball.

Intelligence and Play

Apes are the most intelligent non-human primates. As with birds and other animals, the more intelligent an animal is, the more likely it is to be playful.

While adult macaques rarely make snowballs, they sometimes play with one that a juvenile left behind.

Ape Antics

Young gorillas play wrestle in trees and on the ground, grabbing, slapping, and play biting each other. They also like to hang upside down and swing from branches. They have been observed playing games with grapefruit-size fruit that they kick, throw, or whack with a branch. Gorillas begin to play as babies. One of their first fun activities is sliding down their mother's huge belly, then climbing back up for another fun ride.

World famous scientist and conservationist Dr. Dian Fossey described many play activities of these apes in her book, *Gorillas in the Mist.* Fossey observed a young gorilla slapping

These young western gorillas seem to enjoy playing together.

its chin in rhythm, then a second one joined in by clapping hands, while three other juveniles twirled around playfully. She also watched a group of four young gorillas follow an adult who led the group down a mountain slope, with each gorilla grabbing a tree, spinning around it and then going downward to "dance" with the next tree. When they reached the bottom, all five gorillas piled on top of each other. They repeated this wild game many times with leaves and branches flying in all directions.

Chimpanzees are the most playful apes. They have many play signals, including a sound they make that is similar to human laughter. They may chase each other around a tree, tickle and nibble each other, spin around while dangling from a branch by one arm, jump over each other's backs, and do somersaults. Between play activities, they sometimes groom each other, removing bugs from the play partner's fur.

Some chimpanzee mothers play a game with their young where they repeatedly pretend to leave and then come back. This seems to strengthen the mother-infant bond. Chimpanzees also play with objects such as a stick, a leaf, or a blade of grass. Some of the skills they learn in manipulating these objects can later be helpful in catching ants by dipping a stick into their nest and pulling out prey that cling to the stick, or in sponging up termites with a leaf.

Orangutans play bite, pull hair, and wrestle with each other. While most apes play only with other young of their own species, baboons sometimes play with other species. They have been observed playing in the wild with chimpanzees, velvet monkeys, and even impalas—a type of African antelope.

Three chimpanzees are play chasing in a tree. They also like to play on the ground.

The Value of Play

Interactions with other animals can be helpful in creating a bond, which later leads to jointly defeating an enemy or capturing prey. These encounters may help establish roles and responsibilities within the group and define acceptable behavior toward other group members. Play contacts also teach primates and many other young animals behaviors that will later help them win a mate.

Humans have the largest brains and the greatest intelligence of all species, and they are the most playful of all animals on earth. Dr. Stuart L. Brown, a psychiatrist who has studied the effects of play on human children, feels that play may be as important to humans and other animals as sleeping and dreaming. Besides helping animals develop physical and mental skills, play teaches them how to interact with other animals.

Only in recent times have scientists learned to value play. They study how animals play and determine what skills they learn from these activities. Humans and other young primates play the most because they have well-developed brains and one or both parents look out for their safety. These animals are also fed by their parents, so they have more time to play.

These foals nuzzle and groom each other. Joint play activities help them bond.

Chapter Five

Other Mammals at Play

Manes and tails flying, two wild **foals** race back and forth in a mountain meadow. They often toss their heads, whinny with excitement, and bump into each other playfully. The young horses stop to sniff each other, then gallop off again, often reversing roles of the chasing and the fleeing foal. After a rest, they neck wrestle, while each one uses its teeth to grab some hair from the play partner's mane. Later there's a wrestling match with each foal rearing up on hind legs to push the other with its front legs.

Other Hoofed Animals Play a Lot

Mountain goats, sheep, gazelles, and llamas like to play fight while standing on hind legs, poking and pushing at each other with their front legs. Llamas also spit at each other while play fighting. Cattle, goats, sheep, antelope, and buffalo may jump with front legs onto another young animal's back and ride it. Young mountain sheep like to slide down steep hills, and they often run and romp in groups with adults also joining in.

Young goats are extremely playful, both by themselves and with a play partner. They especially like to leap high and turn halfway around while in the air, tossing their heads and kicking up their heels. Young **kids** like to run off fast and stop suddenly, and they often run in different directions. They whirl around in a circle and sometimes fall down. Young goats jump

over rocks, chase fallen leaves, and toss a small branch into the air many times. They also butt heads and bump bodies with a play partner, and they play "king of the mountain." Kids and lambs both like to jump onto their mother's back and off again. Some young males also horn wrestle. Both goats and sheep do a skipping dance when excited.

Deer run, jump, box with their front legs, and chase each other, taking turns chasing and fleeing. Sometimes they circle a tree at high speed and play "tag." Deer that live in a group often play running games together, with both adults and young taking part. A **fawn** that accidentally somersaulted when it charged at a bush kept on somersaulting now and then for several weeks.

Two mountain goat kids are playing. One is leaping and the other has lowered its head for a mock charge.

African elephant calves are trunk wrestling. Each calf tries to push the other one back with its trunk.

Moose like to run in different directions, and they seem to enjoy splashing through water. Besides playing running games, zebras neck wrestle and so do giraffes. Zebras also play bite each other's necks and kick each other in a play fight.

Hippo calves do underwater flips. As heavy as they are, both young hippos and rhinos leap into the air while twisting their bodies. They also chase each other, and do some pushing, shoving, and play slapping while young. Like humans and many other mammals, hoofed animals first play by themselves and, as they get older, they also play in pairs or groups.

46

Elephants are very playful and begin to play shortly after they are born. Many continue some play activities as adults. Calves run and charge, wrestle with head, mouth, and trunk, and push, roll, and slap each other with their trunks. When play activities get too rough, the mother of one young elephant or another adult female will break them up.

Young camels are especially playful, and they like to leap, roll, and chase each other. Giraffes use their long necks to hit each other playfully. They also wrap their necks around each other to keep the play partner from hitting.

Canines at Play

Most canines engage in a variety of play activities while young, and many continue some play as adults. Anyone who has raised a puppy knows how playful young domestic dogs are, and their young wild relatives are equally playful. Wolves, coyotes, wild dogs, and foxes often use a play bow to invite another pup to play. Another play invitation is given when a pup races off, then comes right back and waits, doing this several times in a row. A third canine play signal is the "leap, leap" when a pup makes two high leaps close together.

Young giraffes engage in play fighting.

47

This photograph shows the enthusiastic play fighting of two wild African dogs.

Canines may growl while wrestling and rolling together on the ground. However, in a play fight their teeth are always covered. Baring one's teeth shows anger, and it indicates that a real fight may be about to start. Sometimes play partners stop in the middle of a bout, and one will make a play bow or give another signal that shows that this is still play. Frequent short rests also assure the partner that this is not a fight.

Wolves play fight, chase each other, and they like to play "keep away" with a stick or bone. A pack of wolves was observed playing "king of the mountain" in a lake, with one wolf trying to stay on a stone and the rest of the pack trying to push it into the water. These play activities are usually accompanied by lots of yelping and barking.

Fox pups jump onto their mother's back and swat at her. They play fight with other pups, biting gently and wrestling. They also chase each other, taking turns being the pursuer. Young foxes dance with their hind legs while keeping their front legs standing still. While play fighting, a fox's ears stand up straight. During a real fight, the fox's ears lie flat. When a

Food Affects Playfulness

Many wild animals are especially playful after making a kill and eating a big meal. Wild African hunting dogs play with leftovers from a kill. They may play tug-of-war with a piece of hide or play chase with one dog running off with a bone and the others chasing after it. Animals that are hungry or thirsty are less likely to play. They may stop playing until things get better.

fox has had enough play, it rolls onto its back and sticks all four legs up in the air.

Foxes and wolves may also play with animals from other species. A researcher has observed a fox being pursued by a herd of caribou. The fox kept coming back for more play chasing. A wolf and bear were seen playing together with the bear putting its arms around the wolf without hurting it. The wolf returned several days in a row for more play.

The gray wolf is playing with a branch.

When play fighting, a **jackal**, or wild dog, may jump into the air, turn its body halfway around, and come down, slamming its rear into the play partner. Later, it will use this maneuver to chase away a vulture or eagle that is feasting at a kill.

Playful Cats, Bears, and Other Mammals

Cats of all kinds are playful while young and may continue some play activities as adults. They like to play with objects, with other cats, and with live or dead prey. Except when playing with their prey, cats' claws are usually drawn in. While wrestling, cats play bite, pull each other's legs, swat with a paw, and roll around on the ground. If one play partner is stronger, it will hold back or self-handicap in order to make the match more even. When lion cubs chase each other, the animal in back will often swat at the legs of the one it is chasing. An adult lioness uses this same motion in order to bring down fast moving prey, such as a gazelle or antelope.

Polar bears dance alone and in pairs. They also play box and nibble each other's bodies. They dig in snow with their snouts and paws and chase each other on land and in water. Bears like to play with objects, such as a stick, rock, or fish. They also chase each other and rear up to knock the play partner off balance, wrestle and roll on the ground, and some actually butt heads.

Young kangaroos play by themselves hopping back and forth, hopping around their mother in a circle, and leaping

into the air. Some also play fight with a partner, when they wrestle, box, and push each other. Young gray kangaroos especially like to play fight with their mothers.

Lion cubs in the African Serengeti Plain are play fighting.

Bats are the only mammals that fly, and young bats play while flying in small or large groups. They romp, tussle, chase each other, slap at each other with their wings, and hold mock battles. Young bats also sniff each other, play bite, and play fight while hanging upside down in a **crèche**, or nursery, where some adults care for them.

Young mice, rats, squirrels, and other rodents are playful animals. They sniff, nuzzle, chase each other, and play fight. Columbian ground squirrels like to chase and jump on each other, do somersaults, and even play leapfrog.

Eastern gray kangaroos learn survival skills from play fighting.

Whether squirrels play chase, a crow slides down a steep, snowy roof, a dolphin plays with a bubble ring it has made, two fox pups wrestle, some young monkeys play "king of the mountain," or a group of children play "store," all these young animals play because they enjoy the activity. Play, however, also has many other benefits. It helps young animals to prepare for adult life. Play helps to develop the skills and strength they will need to capture and hold onto prey, escape from a predator, or win a mate. It also helps animals develop their brains and teaches them about their own bodies and those of other animals. Playing helps many animals to make friends with others in their group.

Glossary

boar—a wild pig

bond—to hold together or to unite two or more individuals

breach—a whale's leap out of the water, followed by falling back in on its side

canine—any animal of the dog family, including wolves, jackals, hyenas, coyotes, and foxes

crèche—a place where young animals live in a group and are cared for by adults

dive-bomb—to fly very fast and straight at an object or toward the ground

fawn—a young deer

foal—a young horse, mule, or other related animal

frolicking—playing happily

imbedded—partly or fully buried in something

jackal—a wild dog that hunts in a pack

jostle—to bump or push

juvenile—young, not yet an adult

kelp—a type of seaweed

kid—a young goat

kit—a young beaver

lemur—a monkeylike primate that can only be found on the Island of Madagascar, near the coast of Africa

motor play—play that involves motion and that is often done alone

object play—playing with a toy, food, or other object

play bow—a play signal that invites another animal to play

predator—an animal that hunts or catches another animal for food

prey—an animal that is hunted or caught for food

primate—an animal from a group of mammals with highly developed brains, forward-looking eyes and well-developed hands. Humans, apes, monkeys and lemurs are primates.

rollover—rolling onto the back and then straightening up again

self-handicap—to hold back one's strength to make a more even match

social play—two or more animals playing together

To Find Out More

Books

Arnosky, Jim. *Field Trips: Bug Hunting, Animal Tracking, Bird-Watching, and Shore Walking*. New York: HarperCollins Publishers, 2002.

Benyus, Janine. *The Secret Language and Remarkable Behavior of Animals*. New York: Black Dog and Leventhal Publishers, Inc., 1998.

Darling, Kathy. *The Elephant Hospital*. Brookfield, CT: Millbrook Press, Inc., 2002.

Tatham, Betty. *How Animals Communicate*. Danbury, CT: Franklin Watts, 2004.

Tatham, Betty. *How Animals Shed Their Skin*. Danbury, CT: Franklin Watts, 2002.

Videos

African Wildlife. National Geographic Video, 1997.

Among the Wild Chimpanzees. National Geographic Video, 1997.

Organizations and Online Sites

American Museum of Natural History
Central Park West at 79th Street
New York, NY 10024-5192
http://www.amnh.org/exhibitions/permanent/ocean/
This site offers information about ocean life, ecosystems, dioramas, and exhibits.

Kids Go Wild
http://www.kidsgowild.com
Conservation is the major theme of this online site that provides young people with facts about animals and offers games. It is sponsored by the Wildlife Conservation Society.

National Geographic Society
http://www.nationalgeographic.com
A wealth of information about animals and science is available on this online site, which includes a section for young people.

Smithsonian Institution
National Museum of Natural History
10th Street and Constitution Ave., NW
Washington, D.C. 20560
http://www.mnh.si.edu/
This online site provides a virtual tour of exhibits and you can learn more about the animals discussed in this book.

Worldwide Whale Web Site
http://www.worldwidewhale.com/index.html
This site is dedicated to whales and dolphins and the people who fight to save them. It includes many facts about these mammals and how they are threatened, and shows ways to protect them.

A Note on Sources

One of the things I like best about doing author visits to schools is the helpful input I get from students. When I asked young readers to help me select subjects to write about, there was a lot of enthusiasm for a book on how animals play. Before selecting a subject, however, I always go first to the Free Public Library near my home to see what has already been written about that topic.

I found quite a few books on animal play for very young children, especially about domestic animals, such as cats and dogs, and also about monkeys. I couldn't find a book that described the play activities of many different animals that live in the wild, neither in the juvenile nor the adult section of the library, nor in the Interlibrary Loan System. That made me want to write this book even more, but the lack of sufficient reference information almost made me give up.

Fortunately, I found Dr. Robert Fagan's college level textbook, *Animal Play Behavior*, at the Biology Library of Princeton University. Dr. Fagan is one of the world's most respected authorities on animal play, and I was very grateful to have access to this wonderful reference book. As usual, my biologist friend Doug Wechsler read and critiqued the manuscript before I sent it to my editor at Franklin Watts. There, a content expert checked the book for scientific accuracy, and my editor reviewed it, making helpful suggestions.

—*Betty Tatham*

Index

Numbers in *italics* indicate illustrations.

About the Author

Betty Tatham directed three YWCAs for a total of twenty-four years before she retired in 2003. Her time is now devoted to writing for children and making school visits. She wrote the award-winning science book, *Penguin Chick*, which was selected as a Book of the Year by Bank Street College of Education and as an Outstanding Science Trade Book by the National Science Teachers Association. The book was on the 2003 Children's Literature Choice List. For Scholastic Library Publishing, Betty has written several titles for the Watts Library series, including *How Animals Shed Their Skin* and *How Animals Communicate*. She lives in Holland, Pennsylvania, with her husband Win.

YOUNG DISCOVERERS

ENERGY AND POWER

ROSIE HARLOW & SALLY MORGAN

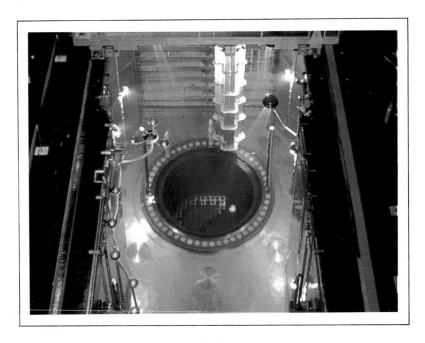

Kingfisher

NEW YORK

KINGFISHER
Larousse Kingfisher Chambers Inc.
95 Madison Avenue
New York, New York 10016

First American edition 1995
10 9 8 7 6 5 4 3 2 1 (PB)
10 9 8 7 6 5 4 3 2 1 (RLB)
Copyright © Larousse plc 1995
All rights reserved under International and
Pan-American Copyright Conventions

LIBRARY OF CONGRESS CATALOGING-IN-
PUBLICATION DATA
Harlow, Rosie.
Energy and power/Rosie Harlow,
Sally Morgan.—1st American ed.
p. cm.—(Young discoverers)
Includes bibliographical references
and Index.
1. Power resources—Juvenile literature.
[1. Power resources. 2. Power resources
—Experiments. 3. Experiments.]
I. Morgan, Sally. II. Title. III. Series.
TJ163.23.H37 1995 333.79—dc20
95-6370 CIP AC

ISBN 1-85697-609-2 (PB)
ISBN 1-85697-610-6 (RLB)

Editor: Jilly MacLeod
Designer: Ben White
Art editor: Val Wright
Photo research: Elaine Willis
Cover design: John Jamieson and
    Shaun Barlow
Illustrations: Derek Brazell p. 26-27 (bot.);
    Richard Draper p. 4-5 (bot.), 6 (right),
    23 (top), 29 (bot.), 30-31; Chris Forsey
    p.8, 10-11, 12-13 (bot.), 14 (left),
    17 (top), 24; Richard Ward p. 5 (top),
    6 (left), 7, 9, 12 (left), 13 (top and
    bot. right), 14 (top), 15, 16, 17 (bot.),
    18-19, 20-21, 22-23 (bot.), 25, 28,
    29 (top)
Photographs: Ecoscene p. 7, 9 (Morgan),
    20 (Glover), 22 (Cooper), 24
    (Winkley), 25 (Jones); Robert Harding
    Picture Library p.12; NHPA p. 31
    (E. Soder); Panos Pictures p. 10, 14
    (R Giling); Science Photo Library p. 4
    (G. Garradd), 8 (D. Lovegrove), 17
    (U.S. Dept. of Energy), 19 (H. Morgan),
    23 (M. Bond); ZEFA p. 5, 27 (J. Blanco)

Printed in Spain

About This Book

This book looks at energy and power and explains how we are damaging our environment by using too much of it. It suggests lots of experiments and things to look out for, as well as ways we can help to make our world a cleaner and safer place.

You should be able to find nearly everything you need for the experiments in and around your home. Be sure to ask an adult to help you when we suggest doing so—some of the experiments could be dangerous to do on your own.

Activity Hints
- Before you begin an experiment, read through the instructions carefully and collect all the things you need.
- When you have finished, clear everything away, especially sharp scissors, and wash your hands.

- Start a special notebook so you can keep a record of what you do in each experiment and the things you find out.

Contents

What is Energy?

Energy is everywhere. We can see it as light, hear it as sound, and feel it as heat. There are other forms of energy as well, such as electrical, chemical, and movement energy. We use electrical energy for power in our homes and chemical energy, in the form of fuel, to power our cars. But, as you will see, when we use energy, we often do harm to our environment as well.

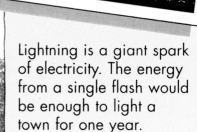

Lightning is a giant spark of electricity. The energy from a single flash would be enough to light a town for one year.

factory

bicycles

tanker

house

We use electrical energy to heat and light factories, offices, schools, and homes. Electricity is also used to light up our streets at night.

4

Do it yourself

See how energy can be used to make things turn. You must ask an adult to help you when you light the candle.

1. Draw a snake, like the one shown here, on a piece of paper. Cut it out and add a red tongue and two eyes. Then tie a length of thread onto the snake's head.

2. Hang your snake above a lighted candle, keeping its tail away from the flame. Now watch it turn. (Be sure to blow out the candle when you have finished.)

How It Works

When a candle burns, two forms of energy are created —heat and light. The heat causes the air to rise up, which in turn makes the snake spin around.

pen

red tongue

colored paper

scissors

candle

office building

truck

street lighting

cars

The energy needed to turn the pedals of a bicycle comes from the cyclist. Cars and trucks get their energy from gasoline and diesel fuel, and some homes are heated using fuel oil. These fuels are delivered in special vehicles called tankers.

gas station

Food for Energy

People use energy to move, keep warm, grow, and stay healthy. The energy we need comes from the food we eat.

5

Generating Power

Energy can be changed from one form into another. For example, when electricity passes through a light bulb, electrical energy is changed into heat and light energy. Most of the electricity we use today is made in power plants. But power plants need a source of energy, too. This usually comes from fuels such as oil, gas, and coal. Inside the power plant, the chemical energy in the fuel is changed into electrical energy.

cooling tower cools steam

boiler

steam

cables carry electricity

tower

steam spins turbine

generator makes electricity

coal supply

👁 Eye-Spy

Use the energy in your muscles to light up a bulb by fitting a generator light set to your bike. When you ride your bike, the wheels turn and the generator makes electricity.

At a power plant, coal is burned inside a boiler. The heat turns water into steam, which is used to spin a special wheel called a turbine. This in turn drives a machine called a generator, which changes the movement energy into electrical energy. Power lines carry the electricity to homes and factories.

Do it yourself

Make your own steam turbine. You'll need an adult to help you.

1. Cut a circle 3 inches across from a thick foil food tray. Pierce a small hole in the center, then snip in toward the hole with your scissors as shown. Twist the sections slightly to make the blades.

2. Ask an adult to punch two small holes in the top of a full, soda can—one in the center, the other about half an inch to one side. Empty the soda out and pour half a cup of water into the can.

Many power plants have cooling towers. The hot steam cools inside the towers and turns back into water. The water is then pumped back to the boiler where it is heated all over again.

3. To make the stand, cut a piece of thick foil 8 in. long and $1\frac{1}{2}$ in. wide. Fold in half lengthwise, then bend into shape as shown so it fits across the top of the can. Make a small hole 2 in. up on each side of the stand.

4. Fix the stand onto the can with a small screw. Then push a 4-inch-long wooden skewer through the holes in the sides of the stand, threading the wheel in place as you go.

5. Make sure the blades of the wheel are positioned over the small hole in the can. Then ask an adult to put your turbine on a stove burner over a low heat. As the water starts to boil, the escaping steam will spin the wheel on your turbine.

soda can

screw

wooden skewer

stand

blades of wheel

heat

The Price of Power

When fuels are burned to give energy, they release harmful gases that pollute (poison) our air. Often these gases lie above cities, creating a layer of smog (dirty air). Some of the gases mix with water in the air to form acids. When it rains, the acid in the rain damages forests and lakes. Burning fuel also releases the gas carbon dioxide. This is called a "greenhouse gas" because it traps the Sun's heat in the atmosphere (the air around the Earth), just like glass traps heat in a greenhouse. The trapped heat makes the atmosphere warm up, which may cause changes in our weather.

Many children suffer from an illness called asthma. They find it hard to breathe and have to use an inhaler. Doctors think that air pollution may be causing the asthma.

Then and Now

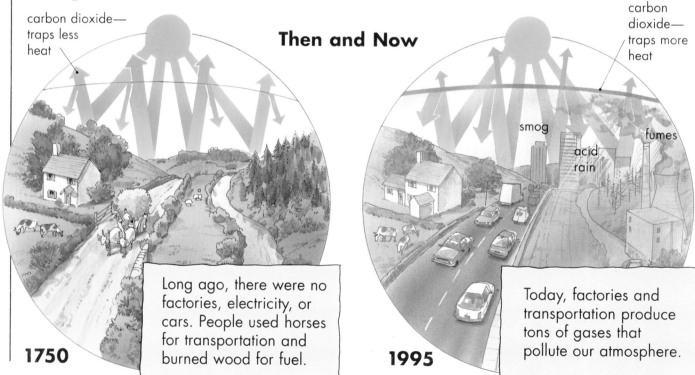

carbon dioxide—traps less heat

carbon dioxide—traps more heat

smog

acid rain

fumes

1750

Long ago, there were no factories, electricity, or cars. People used horses for transportation and burned wood for fuel.

1995

Today, factories and transportation produce tons of gases that pollute our atmosphere.

Do it yourself

Try making smog in a glass jar. You'll need to ask an adult to light the paper for you.

1. Find a large jar and wash it out with water. Don't dry the jar though—you want it to be slightly damp.

A thick layer of smog hangs over New York City making it difficult to see the buildings clearly.

ice

twist of paper

foil

damp jar

smog

How It Works

The smoke from the burning paper rises up in the warm air. When it reaches the cold air around the ice, it sinks back down to the middle where it mixes with the water in the air to form smog. When the weather is damp and warm, the same thing happens over cities that produce a lot of smoke and pollution.

2. Cut a piece of aluminum foil slightly larger than the top of your jar. Put some ice cubes onto the foil.

3. Cut a small piece of newspaper. Fold it a couple of times then twist it up.

4. Ask an adult to light the paper and drop it in the jar. Quickly seal the jar with the foil and ice and watch what happens. (Don't worry if the flame goes out.)

9

The Car Crisis

The car is our most popular form of transportation. Every day across the world, more than 100,000 new cars appear on the roads. But every time we use a car, we add more pollution to the atmosphere. This pollution is particularly bad in cities where rush hour traffic fills the streets. It is caused by the cars' exhaust fumes, which are made up of harmful gases such as sulfur dioxide, carbon monoxide, and nitrogen oxides. They also contain tiny bits of soot. To cut down on air pollution we must design cars that are cleaner to run, and use our cars less often.

Rush hour traffic in Bangkok, Thailand, produces so much pollution that a dirty layer of smog hangs over the city.

How Can We Help?

- Walk or use a bicycle on short journeys.
- Use public transportation instead of a car as much as possible.
- On regular journeys, see if your family can pair up with another family and use one car instead of two.

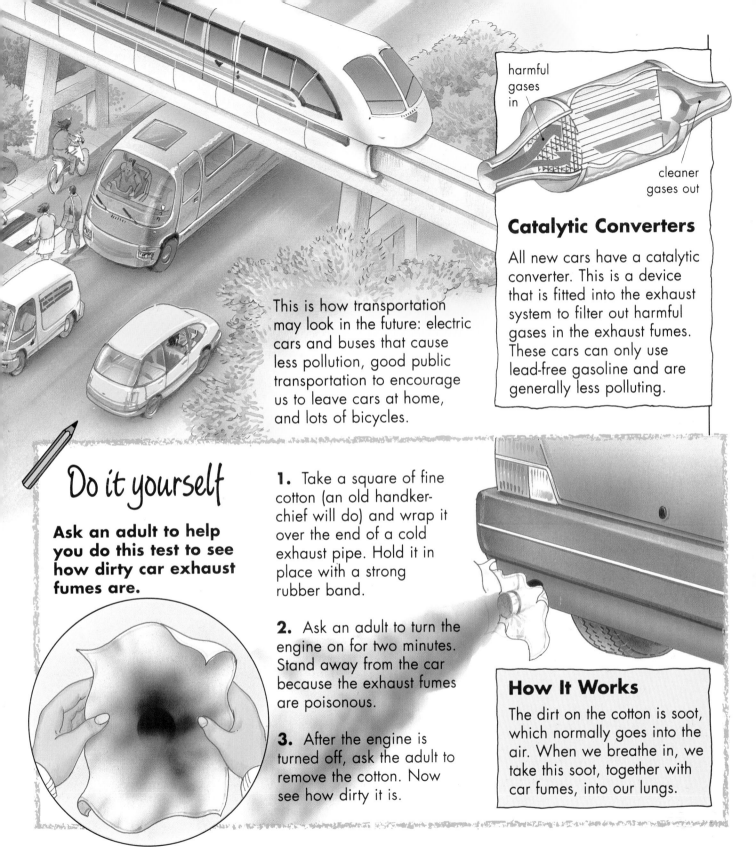

harmful
gases
in

cleaner
gases out

Catalytic Converters

All new cars have a catalytic converter. This is a device that is fitted into the exhaust system to filter out harmful gases in the exhaust fumes. These cars can only use lead-free gasoline and are generally less polluting.

This is how transportation may look in the future: electric cars and buses that cause less pollution, good public transportation to encourage us to leave cars at home, and lots of bicycles.

Do it yourself

Ask an adult to help you do this test to see how dirty car exhaust fumes are.

1. Take a square of fine cotton (an old handkerchief will do) and wrap it over the end of a cold exhaust pipe. Hold it in place with a strong rubber band.

2. Ask an adult to turn the engine on for two minutes. Stand away from the car because the exhaust fumes are poisonous.

3. After the engine is turned off, ask the adult to remove the cotton. Now see how dirty it is.

How It Works

The dirt on the cotton is soot, which normally goes into the air. When we breathe in, we take this soot, together with car fumes, into our lungs.

11

Nature's Fuels

All living things depend on the Sun for energy. Plants use light energy to make their own food—a form of chemical energy. Animals eat plants so they can use the chemical energy stored inside. The fuels we all depend on—coal, gas, and oil—also contain a store of chemical energy. They are called "fossil" fuels because their energy comes from organisms (plants and animals) that lived millions of years ago. When the organisms died their bodies became buried and their remains slowly turned into coal, gas, and oil.

Oil Underground

Oil is the fossil remains of tiny animals that died millions of years ago. Oil rigs drill down below the ground or seabed and remove the oil.

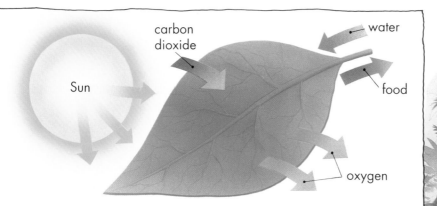

carbon dioxide

water

Sun

food

oxygen

Energy from the Sun

Plants capture light energy from the Sun and use it to make food in a process called photosynthesis. Inside the leaves, the gas carbon dioxide is combined with water to make sugars and a substance called starch. The gas oxygen is produced and released back into the air.

Do it yourself

Do this simple experiment to see whether or not plants need light to grow.

1. Put some damp cotton balls on three glass jar lids and sprinkle a few alfalfa sprout seeds on top.

2. Put one lid on a sunny windowsill, another in a dark cupboard. Cut a small hole in a cardboard box and put the third lid inside. Close up the box.

3. Leave the seeds to grow for a week, keeping the cotton wool damp with a little water.

How It Works

The seeds on the window-sill grow well because they have enough light. Those in the cupboard shrivel and die because, without light, they cannot make food and grow. The seeds in the box grow toward the hole to get as much light as possible.

Coal is the remains of plants that lived in swamps millions of years ago. As the plants died, they sunk layer upon layer beneath the water. The weight of the top layers squashed the bottom layer which eventually became much harder, forming coal.

coal seam

👁 Eye-Spy

Next time you eat bread, cereal, potatoes, pasta, or rice, think about where the food has come from. All these foods contain starch made by plants from the Sun's energy.

13

Other Natural Fuels

Coal, oil, and gas are not the only fuels that nature gives us. In some parts of the world, such as Ireland and Siberia, people still use a substance called peat. Peat is the first stage in the long coal-making process. It is softer than coal and not as rich in energy, but it can be burned for fuel and is sometimes used in power plants to generate electricity. Wood also makes a good fuel—many people still use it to heat their homes and for cooking.

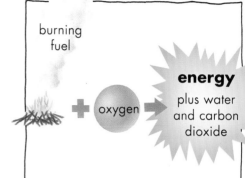

burning fuel + oxygen → **energy** plus water and carbon dioxide

How Fuels Burn

As we have seen, fuels contain a store of chemical energy. When fuels burn, they react with oxygen in the air and release heat and light energy, plus water and carbon dioxide. The proper word to describe something burning in air is combustion.

Wood is an important fuel in poor countries, where it is collected and burned on fires and stoves for cooking food and boiling water.

Digging for Fuel

Peat is still an important fuel in Ireland, where it is dug up from the ground as small bricklike pieces. The peat bricks are then dried before being burned on fires and stoves in the home.

Low on Fuels

Unfortunately, there is only a limited amount of fossil fuels in the world. Once the supplies have run out they cannot be replaced. This is why fossil fuels are called nonrenewable fuels. Wood is also being used up too quickly. Trees can be replanted but they still take over 50 years to grow. So we need to find alternative sources of energy if we are not to run out of power.

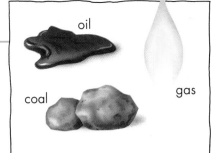

oil

gas

coal

How Much Is Left?

There may be enough coal to last for another 300 years. But oil and gas may run out within the next 50 years.

Do it yourself

Make some paper logs to burn as fuel.

1. Tear some newspaper into strips and put them in a large bowl of hot water. Mash the paper into a pulp with a wooden spoon.

2. Scoop up the pulp using a sieve. Pick up a handful of pulp and squeeze out all the water, forming a log shape as you do so.

3. Make several more logs, then leave them to dry out. Then ask an adult to help you make a fire with them.

How Can We Help?

If we all use less energy then the supply of fossil fuels will last longer. Try to turn off unwanted lights, use the car less often, and wear an extra sweater instead of turning the heat up.

newspaper strips

squeeze the water out

paper logs

15

Splitting Atoms

Instead of using fossil fuels to make electricity, we can use "nuclear power." The energy for nuclear power comes from a metal called uranium. Like all matter, uranium is made up of tiny particles called atoms. When a uranium atom is split into smaller particles, a vast amount of heat energy is released. This can be used to generate electricity. But waste products from nuclear power plants are very dangerous and are difficult to get rid of safely.

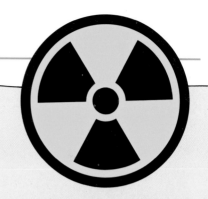

Radioactive Waste

Nuclear power produces a dangerous form of energy called radioactivity. This can contaminate (infect) people and animals, making them very sick. Radioactive waste from power plants is marked with this warning symbol.

Energy from Atoms

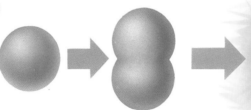

neutron fired at atom

atom splits

heat energy produced

neutrons released

Sun's surface

In a nuclear reaction, tiny particles called neutrons are fired at uranium atoms at very high speeds. They split the uranium atoms, causing them to release more neutrons and lots of heat energy. The neutrons bump into more uranium atoms, causing them to split. This is called a fission reaction. Another type of nuclear reaction, called nuclear fusion, is taking place inside the Sun all the time.

If there has been a leak at a nuclear power plant, scientists use a machine called a Geiger counter to test for radioactivity in the ground and in animals. Sometimes farmers paint their sheep yellow to show they have been contaminated with radioactivity.

The reactor core in a nuclear power plant is surrounded by water. The water is heated by the nuclear reaction.

Making Electricity

In a nuclear power plant, the uranium is placed in rods inside a "reactor core." It is carefully shielded so that the radioactivity cannot escape. The heat from the nuclear reaction heats the water surrounding the core. This hot water is then used to turn water in the heat exchanger into steam. The steam is used to spin the turbines, and electricity is generated.

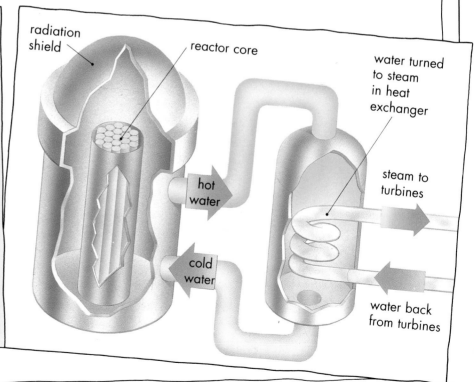

radiation shield

reactor core

water turned to steam in heat exchanger

hot water

steam to turbines

cold water

water back from turbines

Energy from the Sun

The Sun is like a huge power plant, releasing vast amounts of heat and light energy. It supplies a free source of energy that will not run out. Scientists have devised many new ways of making use of solar energy. Solar panels absorb heat from the Sun and heat water for homes and factories. Other panels, called photovoltaics, can change light directly into electricity. Both of these ways of using solar energy produce very little pollution.

👁 Eye-Spy

On a hot sunny day, a garden hose acts like a solar panel. It absorbs the Sun's energy and the water inside heats up. Look out for a cat lying on a hose, enjoying the heat.

Do it yourself

Make some tea using energy from the Sun.

1. Take two clear glass bottles the same size. Paint one of them black. Put two tea bags in each bottle and fill them up with cold water.

2. Put the bottles on a sunny windowsill for at least six hours. If you have a thermometer, test the temperature of the water every two hours to see which bottle heats up quickest. Watch the water turn brown as your tea brews.

tea bags

water

thermometer

How It Works

The Sun's energy heats the water and brews the tea. Because the black glass absorbs heat better than the clear glass, the water in the black bottle will heat up faster and the tea will brew more quickly.

18

Trapping the Sun's Energy

Simple solar panels, like the one in the diagram, are placed on the roof of a house and used to heat water. The water absorbs heat as it circulates through the pipes in the panel and becomes much hotter.

On a much larger scale, this solar power plant in California does the same thing. Thousands of mirrors reflect the sunlight onto tubes containing a special oil. The oil is heated to 1067°F (575°C) and is used to make steam which, in turn, spins a turbine to make electricity.

glass

cold water in

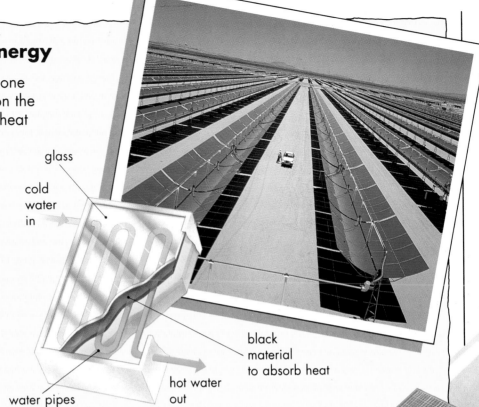

black material to absorb heat

hot water out

water pipes

Called the Sunraycer, this strange-looking car is powered by solar energy. It won the first international solar-powered car race in 1987, traveling more than 1,950 miles (3,140km) across Australia.

 **Eye-Spy**

Look out for small items powered by solar energy, such as calculators, watches, and radios. They use photovoltaic cells to convert the light energy into electricity.

19

Wind Power

The wind is another free source of energy that can be trapped and used to make electricity. People have made use of wind power for hundreds of years. Windmills were once built to turn a large millstone that was used to grind wheat into flour. Small wind-powered pumps are still used to pump water from wells. About 25 years ago, the first modern wind generators appeared in the United States. Since then, many more have been built all around the world. Because the wind will never stop blowing, wind power is an important source of renewable energy.

Windmills

Traditional windmills for grinding wheat are still found in countries such as the Netherlands. This windmill has four large sails to catch the wind.

Wind Farms

A collection of wind generators is called a wind farm. This one is in California, on the mountains behind the city of Los Angeles. It is very windy here, so the area is ideal for wind power.

On a wind farm, each generator has two or three long narrow blades. As the blades turn in the wind, they turn a turbine which generates electricity.

Do it yourself

Make this wind-powered winch and see how you can use the power of the wind to lift objects into the air.

1. Tape a thread spool on its side to the top of a length of wood about 10 inches long.

2. Cut four pieces of cardboard—2 inches x 1 inch, for your blades. Tape each blade onto the end of a toothpick as shown. Then stick the other end of the toothpicks into a cork and twist the blades so that they face each other.

3. Stick the cork onto the sharp end of a pencil. Thread the pencil through the thread spool on the wooden stand. Make sure the pencil turns freely in the hole.

4. Jam a slightly smaller thread spool (complete with thread) onto the blunt end of the pencil. If the hole is too big, wind tape around the end of the pencil to give a tight fit.

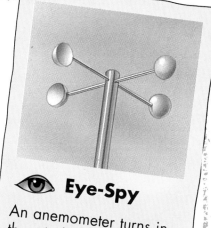

Eye-Spy

An anemometer turns in the wind and is used to measure the wind's speed. See if you can spot one.

materials

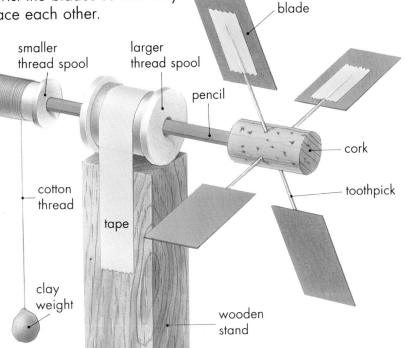

smaller thread spool

larger thread spool

pencil

blade

cork

toothpick

cotton thread

tape

clay weight

wooden stand

5. Unravel about 8 inches of thread from the smaller spool and tie a blob of modeling clay on the end to act as a weight.

6. Blow on the blades to see if your winch can lift the weight. You may need to alter the direction of the blades or make the weight slightly smaller to get your machine to work properly. Now try your machine outside in the wind.

The Power of Water

Moving water is an important source of free energy. Hundreds of years ago people built watermills by rivers and used them to grind wheat into flour, just like a windmill. Today, moving water can be used to generate electricity. Huge dams, called hydroelectric dams, are built across rivers to generate electricity for nearby cities. The waters of the ocean are also moving, and waves and tides are now being used as a source of energy.

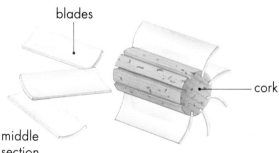

Hydroelectric dams are built across rivers where there is a steep fall in height. The water falling from the top of the dam turns a huge turbine to make electricity.

Do it yourself

Try making your own waterwheel out of a plastic drink bottle. You may need to ask an adult to help you if you find some of the cutting too difficult.

1. Cut a plastic soda bottle into three pieces as shown. The middle section should be 3 inches deep. Now cut four strips, 1 inch wide, out of the middle piece. Cut each strip in half to make eight blades.

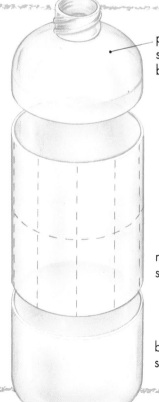

plastic soda bottle

middle section

base section

blades

cork

2. Draw eight lines evenly spaced down the side of a cork. Cut slits down the lines with a blunt knife and push a blade into each slit.

22

turbine

This is a tidal barrage, designed to trap the power of the tides. It is built across the mouth of a river, near the sea. As the tide moves up or down the river, the water passes over a turbine, causing it to turn and generate electricity.

Wave generators (above) are built on the coast. The waves are funneled up a special ramp, forcing air through the turbines to make electricity.

thread wrapped around cork

faucet

water turns wheel

wooden skewer

water

clay

3. Cut away a section of the bottle base as shown. Then pierce two holes just below the rim, one on either side.

4. Cut a wooden skewer in half. Feed each half through a hole and push the sticks into the ends of the cork.

5. Put a second cork on the end of one of the sticks. Tie a length of thread around it and attach a blob of modeling clay. Now put your water-wheel under a faucet. Slowly turn the faucet on and watch your machine lift the weight.

Energy Underground

Hot rocks beneath the Earth's surface have been used as a free source of heat for hundreds of years. Water moving through cracks in the rocks is heated, often to temperatures of up to 660°F (350°C). The hot water can be brought to the surface and used to make electricity. This form of energy is called geothermal energy. It is a very important source of energy in countries such as Iceland and New Zealand.

Sometimes the water and steam heated by the hot rocks burst out of the ground to form geysers and hot springs. In Iceland, everyone heats their homes with water from hot springs.

Hot Rock Power

Geothermal power plants are built in places where there is very hot water in the rocks just below the ground. A pipe is drilled into the rocks to allow steam to escape to the surface, where it is used to drive a turbine and generate electricity for local homes and factories. The waste water is pumped back down into the ground to replace the hot water that has been removed.

hot water up

cold water down

hot rocks

The Wonders of Waste

Garbage could be a cheap source of energy, if only we made more use of it. We have been burying our garbage in holes called landfills for many years. As the waste breaks down it releases a gas called methane. This is often left to escape into the air, but it can be collected and burned to make hot water and electricity for local homes. Or, instead of burying our garbage, we could use it as fuel to make electricity.

In some parts of the world, such as India, animal dung is collected and dried. Then it can be burned on fires for cooking and heating.

Do it yourself

Show that rotting waste gives off a gas.

1. Soak some dried peas or beans in water overnight. Then put them in a clear plastic bag.

2. Squash all the air out of the bag and seal it. Then place the bag somewhere warm and leave it for a week. Now see what has happened. (Throw the bag away without opening it once you have finished the experiment.)

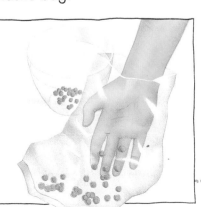

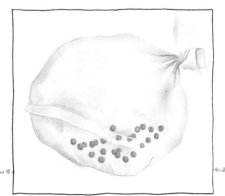

How It Works

The peas or beans soon start to rot as they are broken down by tiny organisms in the air called bacteria. As they rot they give off the gas methane, which causes the bag to blow up.

Energy in the Home

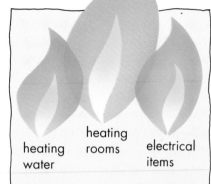

Every home uses energy, but what is it needed for? Modern homes are wired so that electricity can be carried to each room, providing power for lights and items such as televisions and toasters. Fuels such as oil, gas, and coal may also be burned in boilers to provide hot water for central heating and for washing. Some equipment is battery-powered. Batteries are stores of energy which contain chemicals that react together to form an electric current. Some batteries can be recharged many times using a power source such as the Sun or electricity.

heating water   heating rooms   electrical items

Where Does It Go?

More than half the energy we use at home goes to heat rooms. One-fourth is used to power electrical items and one-fifth is used to heat water for washing.

The modern bedroom is very energy-hungry! We use batteries to power toys and run televisions and radios on electricity.

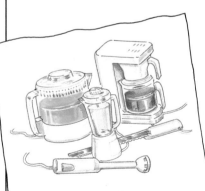

Eye-Spy

Kitchens use up a lot of energy. Can you figure out why? To help you, count the number of electrical items in your kitchen. How many are there compared with your bedroom?

Do it yourself

Do an energy survey in your home to see how much energy you use.

Write down the gas and electricity meter readings. Then go back three hours later to see by how much they have gone up. Take readings at different times of the day and year to see how the amount of energy you use varies.

Heating and lighting also use up energy. But we only need them when it is cold or dark outside.

Many people now have computers at home that may be left on for many hours at a time. Computers use up a lot of electricity.

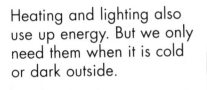

Battery Power

Batteries are a very useful source of energy because they do not have to be wired to the electricity supply. They can be used anywhere to power portable items such as personal stereos. But they do not last very long because the chemicals that power them soon run out.

Save It!

We all use too much energy. If we reduce the amount we use each day we will create less pollution and our fossil fuels will last longer. There are many ways of saving energy in the home. Houses can be built with better "insulation" to stop heat escaping through the walls and roof. Low-energy light bulbs are widely available, and many electrical goods now carry labels telling us how much energy they use so we can buy the most efficient.

👁 Eye-Spy

Does your family use low-energy light bulbs? They last about eight times as long as ordinary light bulbs and use about one-fourth of the electricity.

Do it yourself

Insulation is used to stop heat escaping. Do this simple experiment to see which materials hold heat the longest.

Wrap four bottles in different materials as shown and pour an equal amount of hot water (from the hot faucet) into each one. Take the temperature of the water in each bottle, then take it again after 5 minutes, 10 minutes, and 20 minutes. Which material gives the best insulation? Which would you wear to keep warm?

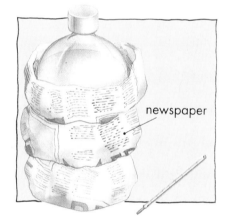

newspaper

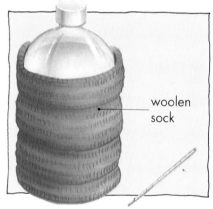

woolen sock

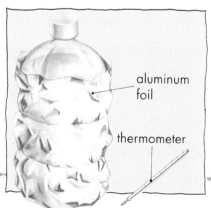

aluminum foil

thermometer

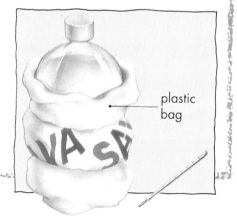

plastic bag

28

Do it yourself

Lots of houses lose heat through drafts. See how drafty your home is with this draft tester.

Cut a square of plastic wrap about 6 inches x 8 inches and tape it to a pencil. Now hold your tester in front of gaps around windows and doors. See if the film is blown around in a draft.

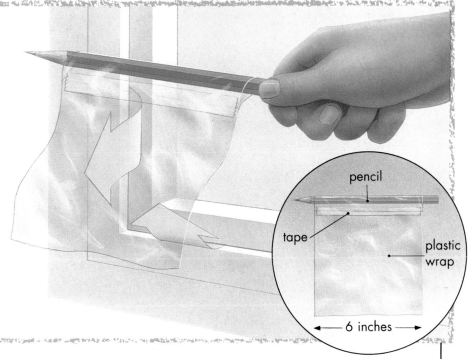

pencil

tape

plastic wrap

← 6 inches →

How Can We Help?

- Make sure our homes are well insulated so heat, and therefore energy, is not wasted.
- Fill up cracks around windows and doors to stop heat being lost through drafts.
- Wear an extra sweater if we are cold instead of turning up the heating.
- Always use low-energy light bulbs.
- Turn lights off when they are not needed.
- Buy electrical goods that use as little energy as possible.

This home is very energy efficient—that is, little energy is wasted. Its grass roof acts as insulation, keeping the heat in, whereas the small pool helps to keep the house cool in summer.

pool

29

Tomorrow's Home

The home of the future may look very different from the ones we live in today. There will be many energy-saving features, as well as ways of making use of free energy sources such as the Sun. The sunny side of the house will have large windows and maybe a sun porch to trap heat energy. There will be solar panels on the roof to trap sunlight, and water pipes underground will pick up heat from the soil.

This house has been designed to use energy as efficiently as possible and to make the most use of free energy sources.

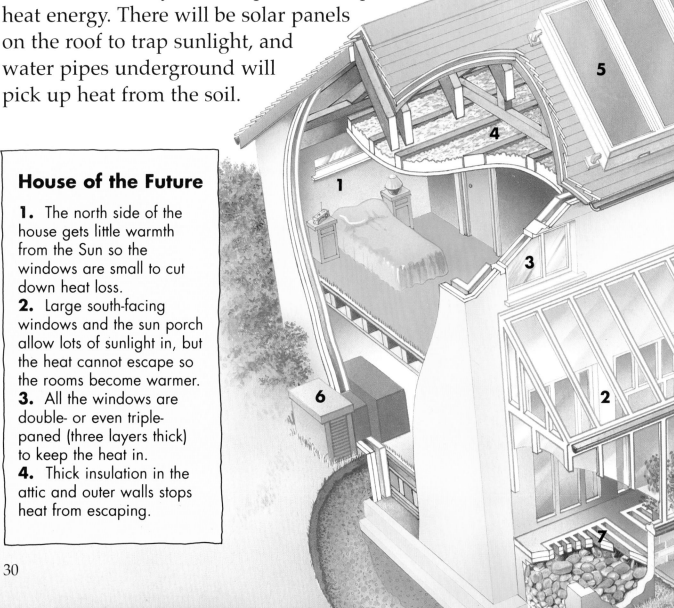

House of the Future

1. The north side of the house gets little warmth from the Sun so the windows are small to cut down heat loss.
2. Large south-facing windows and the sun porch allow lots of sunlight in, but the heat cannot escape so the rooms become warmer.
3. All the windows are double- or even triple-paned (three layers thick) to keep the heat in.
4. Thick insulation in the attic and outer walls stops heat from escaping.

This house in Switzerland has special solar tiles to replace the normal roof tiles. If we use solar power more widely (even in cloudy areas) there will be less need to build new power plants.

Electric cars may be more common in the future. Solar energy could be used to make electricity to recharge the car.

5. Solar panels on the roof trap heat energy and use it to provide the house with plenty of hot water.

6. A heat exchanger pumps water through underground pipes. In winter it is used to absorb heat from the ground to warm the house. In summer it loses heat into the ground to keep the house cool.

7. A heat collector in the ground absorbs heat from the soil which is used to warm the sun porch.

8. The garage is fitted with a car recharger so the car's battery can be recharged overnight.

Index

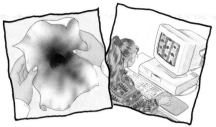

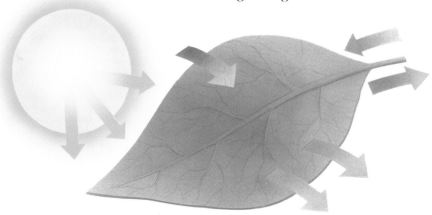